FOOD LOVERS

BABY AND TODDLER

FOOD LOVERS

BABY AND TODDLER

RECIPES SELECTED BY JONNIE LÉGER

Trans
Atlantic
Press

All recipes make four servings, unless otherwise indicated.

The recipes in this book range from simple puréed fruits and vegetables to meals that can be shared by the whole family. ALWAYS consult your doctor or health visitor before introducing new foods to your baby and carefully follow their guidelines about weaning and feeding babies and young children.

For best results when cooking the recipes in this book, buy fresh ingredients and follow the instructions carefully. Make sure that everything is properly cooked through before serving, particularly any meat and shellfish, and note that as a general rule vulnerable groups such as the very young, elderly people, pregnant women, convalescents and anyone suffering from an illness should avoid dishes that contain raw or lightly cooked eggs.

For all recipes, quantities are given in metric measurements followed by the equivalent in standard U.S. cups and imperial measures. Follow one set or the other, but not a mixture of both because conversions may not be exact. Standard spoon and cup measurements are level and are based on the following:

1 tsp. = 5 ml, 1 tbsp. = 15 ml, 1 cup = 250 ml / 8 fl oz.

Note that Australian standard tablespoons are 20 ml, so Australian readers should use 3 tsp. in place of 1 tbsp. when measuring small quantities.

The electric oven temperatures in this book are given for conventional ovens with top and bottom heat. The cooking times given should be used as an approximate guideline only.

CONTENTS

RED LENTIL, CARROT AND TOMATO PURÉE

Ingredients

2 tsp olive oil

½ small onion, chopped

1 large carrot, scrubbed and chopped

75 g / ⅓ cup red lentils

1 tsp tomato paste

Method

Prep and cook time: 1 hour

1 Heat the oil in a large skillet (frying pan), add the onion and cook gently for 5 minutes, until softened but not browned. Add the carrot and continue cooking for another 4–5 minutes.

2 Add the lentils, tomato paste and 475 ml / 2 cups of water. Bring to a boil, reduce heat and simmer for 40–50 minutes, or until the lentils are soft.

3 Drain the mixture, reserving the liquid. Purée the solids in a food processor or blender until smooth, adding the leftover liquid 1 tbsp at a time until the desired consistency is reached. Serve at room temperature.

BROCCOLI AND POTATO PURÉE

Ingredients

250 g / 8 oz potato, peeled and cubed

250 g / 8 oz broccoli, washed and broken into florets

Method

Prep and cook time: 25 min

1 Put the potato into a small pan and add 300ml / 1¼ cups of boiling water. Cook, covered, for 7 minutes or until the potato is becoming tender.

2 Next add the broccoli and cook for 5 minutes until the broccoli is tender.

3 Drain off 150ml / ^{2}/3 cup of the cooking liquid and reserve.

4 Use a stick blender to whiz the broccoli and potatoes together until smooth. Add a little of the reserved cooking liquid to make a really smooth texture, if needed.

BUTTERNUT SQUASH PURÉE

Ingredients

150 g / 5 oz (¼ medium) butternut squash, halved and seeded

Method

Prep and cook time: 50 min

1 Heat the oven to 200C (400F / Gas Mark 6).

2 Place the squash, flesh side down, in an ovenproof dish with 5 tbsp water. Bake until tender, about 40 minutes.

3 Scoop the flesh from the skin and put into a bowl, adding 2 tbsp of hot water or squash cooking liquid. Mash with a fork or stick (immersion) blender to make a smooth consistency, adding more water if needed.

SWEET POTATO PURÉE

Ingredients

1 small sweet potato

Method

Prep and cook time: 50 min

1 Heat the oven to 200C (400F / Gas Mark 6).

2 Pierce the sweet potato several times with a fork and place on a baking sheet. Bake until tender, about 40 minutes.

3 Scoop the potato flesh from the skin and put into a bowl, adding 2 tbsp of hot water. Mash with a fork or stick (immersion) blender to make a smooth consistency, adding more water if needed.

APPLE PURÉE

Ingredients

225 g / 8 oz cooking apple, peeled, cored and sliced

25 g / 2 tbsp superfine (caster) sugar

Apple slices, to garnish

Method
Prep and cook time: 15 min

1 Put the apples into a heatproof bowl with the sugar and 2 tbsp water.

2 Cover with microwave-safe plastic wrap (clingfilm), pierce a few times and cook on High for 4 minutes until soft. Let stand for 2 minutes. Or put all the ingredients in a pan and heat gently until the apples are soft.

3 Using a stick (immersion) blender, blend the apples to a smooth purée. Garnish with apple slices.

BANANA CHOCOLATE FROMAGE BLANC

Ingredients

2 tablespoons chocolate chips

2 ripe bananas

4 tbsp fromage blanc (frais)

To garnish:

Banana slices

Cocoa powder

Method
Prep and cook time: 10 min

1 In a medium microwave-safe bowl, microwave the chocolate chips on medium power, stirring every 20 seconds, just until melted.

2 Slice the bananas directly into the bowl and mash well with a fork until smoothly blended into the chocolate. Stir in the fromage blanc (frais).

3 Garnish with sliced banana and sprinkle with cocoa powder.

AVOCADO DIP
WITH VEGETABLES

Ingredients

1 large ripe avocado, quartered

150 ml / ²/₃ cup sour cream

1 tbsp lime juice

4 carrots, trimmed and cut into sticks

4 celery stalks, trimmed and cut into finger-size sticks

To garnish:

1 cherry tomato, halved

Method
Prep and cook time: 15 min

1 Peel and pit the avocado. Roughly chop the flesh and put into a food processor with the sour cream and lime juice. Pulse until smooth.

2 Spoon the avocado dip into small dish and garnish with the cherry tomato halves. Serve with the carrot and celery sticks.

CARROT SOUP

Ingredients

1 tbsp olive oil

1 small onion, chopped

900 ml / 4 cups boiling water

500 g / 1 lb carrots, roughly chopped

2 tsp honey

To garnish:

2 tbsp plain dried breadcrumbs

1 tsp chopped fresh dill

Method

Prep and cook time: 30 min

1 Heat the oil in a large, heavy pot or Dutch oven. Add the onion and fry gently for 5 minutes until softened but not browned.

2 Add the boiling water, carrots and honey. Cover and simmer for 20 minutes until the carrots are tender.

3 Remove from the heat. Use a stick (immersion) blender to blend the mixture to a semi-smooth purée (or transfer to a blender or food processor). If you know your child prefers it lump-free, continue blending until the soup is really smooth.

4 Serve at room temperature, garnished with a sprinkling of breadcrumbs and dill.

SWEET POTATO AND SQUASH SOUP WITH CHICKEN

Ingredients

2 tomatoes

2 tsp olive oil

1 small onion, chopped

800 ml / 3½ cups vegetable broth (stock) or water

300 g / 12 oz butternut squash, peeled, seeded, and chopped

1 medium sweet potato, peeled and roughly chopped

1 skinless, boneless chicken breast, chopped

Method

Prep and cook time: 40 min

1 Bring a medium saucepan of water to a boil; drop in the tomatoes and heat for 1–3 minutes until the tomato skins split. Remove the tomatoes with a slotted spoon; when cool enough to handle, peel and coarsely chop.

2 Heat the oil in a large saucepan or soup pot; add the onion and fry for a few minutes to soften (do not brown).

3 Add the broth (stock) or water, squash, sweet potato, tomatoes and chicken. Cover and simmer for 15 minutes until the vegetables are soft.

4 Remove a ladleful of the vegetables and reserve. Use a stick (immersion) blender to whiz the rest of the soup to a smooth purée (or transfer in batches to a blender or food processor). Return the reserved vegetables to the soup and serve.

VEGETABLE AND FISH SOUP

Ingredients

2 tsp olive oil

1 onion, chopped

1 potato, cubed

1 large carrot, sliced

125 g / 4 oz fish fillet, cut into chunks

75 g / ½ cup broccoli, cut into small florets

Method

Prep and cook time: 20 min

1 Heat the oil in a large saucepan or soup pot and add the onion. Cook for a few minutes, to soften.

2 Add 600 ml / 2½ cups of water, the potato and carrot. Cover, bring to a boil, reduce the heat and simmer for 10 minutes.

3 Add the fish and broccoli and cook for 5 more minutes.

SOYBEAN SOUP

Ingredients

200 g / 7 oz frozen soy beans

1 leek, sliced (white part only)

1 large carrot, chopped

6 scallions (spring onions) trimmed
and chopped

600 ml / 2½ cups hot vegetable
broth (stock)

To garnish:

1 tbsp chopped parsley

2 tbsp crumbled cheese

Method

Prep and cook time: 30 min

1 Put the frozen soybeans, leek, carrot and scallions (spring onion) into a large saucepan or soup pot with the vegetable broth (stock). Bring to a boil, reduce heat and simmer for 20 minutes until the vegetables are tender.

2 Use a stick blender to make a smooth purée (or transfer in batches to a blender or food processor).

3 Pour into bowls and serve garnished with parsley and crumbled cheese.

RICE WITH VEGETABLES

Ingredients

4 carrots, peeled and shredded

150 g / ¾ cup long-grain rice

1 shallot, finely chopped

50 g / ½ cup finely chopped broccoli

Method

Prep and cook time: 30 min

1 Put the carrots into a large saucepan and add the rice, shallot, broccoli and 300ml / 1¼ cups of water. Bring to a boil, reduce the heat and simmer, covered, for 20 minutes until the rice is tender and the liquid is absorbed.

2 Use a stick (immersion) blender and whiz for a few seconds to make a semi-smooth purée (or transfer to a blender or food processor).

CHICKEN AND PARSNIP PIES

Ingredients

450 g / 1 lb parsnips, peeled and quartered

250 g / ½ lb potatoes, peeled and chopped

1 tbsp olive oil

350 g / 12 oz skinless, boneless chicken breast, cut into chunks

1 small leek, trimmed and finely chopped (white part only)

100 g / ½ cup finely chopped carrot

150 ml / ⅔ cup heavy (double cream)

25 g / 2 tbsp butter

2 tbsp milk

Method

Prep and cook time: 1 hour

1 Heat the oven to 200C (400F / Gas Mark 6).

2 Put the parsnips and potatoes together in a large saucepan with enough salted water to cover. Bring to a boil, reduce the heat and simmer for 20 minutes until tender.

3 Meanwhile, heat the oil in a large skillet (frying pan); add the chicken and fry for 5 minutes. Add the leek and cook for 5 more minutes.

4 Stir in the carrot and cream and warm through. Cook, stirring, until sauce thickens slightly.

5 Drain the potatoes and parsnips; return to the pan and mash until smooth. Beat in the butter and milk.

6 Divide the chicken mixture between 4 individual ovenproof dishes and top each one with one quarter of the potato mixture. Bake for 30 minutes until golden.

ZUCCHINI AND PEA RISOTTO

Ingredients

1 tbsp olive oil

1 small onion, chopped

1 zucchini (courgette), finely chopped

175 g / 1 cup risotto rice

100 g / $^2/_3$ cup frozen green peas

50 g / ½ cup grated Cheddar cheese

Method

Prep and cook time: 35 min

1 Heat the oil in a large deep skillet or soup pot. Add the onion and fry gently for a few minutes to soften (do not brown).

2 Meanwhile, put 900 ml / 4 cups of water on to boil in a saucepan.

3 Add the zucchini to the skillet and cook, stirring, 2 minutes, then stir in the rice. Add 300 ml / 1¼ cups of the boiling water, stir and cook for a few minutes until the liquid is absorbed. Add another 300 ml / 1¼ cups boiling water to the rice and stir from time to time until the liquid is absorbed.

4 Add the peas and the remaining boiling water, stir and simmer until the rice is tender and the liquid is almost absorbed.

5 Remove from the heat and stir in the cheese to serve.

COTTAGE PIE

Ingredients

1 tbsp vegetable oil

2 onions, chopped

450 g / 1 lb ground beef

450 ml / 2 cups beef broth (stock)

1 tbsp all-purpose flour

1 tbsp Worcestershire sauce

1 tbsp tomato purée

Salt and freshly ground pepper, to taste

900 g / 2 lb potatoes, peeled and cut into chunks

25 g / 2 tbsp butter

4 tbsp milk

Method

Prep and cook time: 1 hour 30 min

1 Heat the oven to 170C (325F / Gas Mark 3).

2 Heat the oil in a large flameproof casserole and fry the onions for 5 minutes until softened.

3 Add the beef and cook, stirring, until well browned. Stir in the broth (stock), flour, Worcestershire sauce and tomato purée. Bring to a boil and season with salt and pepper. Cover and carefully transfer to the oven. Bake for 20 minutes, until tender.

4 Meanwhile, put the potatoes into a saucepan with enough salted water to cover. Bring to a boil, reduce the heat and simmer for 20–25 minutes until very tender.

5 Drain the potatoes, return to the pan, and mash until very smooth. Beat in the butter and milk.

6 Increase the oven temperature to 220C (400F / Gas Mark 6).

7 Spoon the beef into a 1.7 liter / 1½-quart baking dish. Spread the potato mixture on top, to completely cover the meat. Place on a baking sheet and bake for 25 minutes or until the top is starting to brown.

COUSCOUS SALAD

Ingredients

1 large carrot, finely diced

1 red bell pepper, deseeded and finely diced

1 yellow bell pepper, deseeded and finely diced

100 g / 4 oz couscous

Juice of 1 orange

½ cucumber, finely chopped

1 stick celery, finely chopped

Method
Prep and cook time: 20 min

1 Put the carrot into a large bowl with 2 tbsp of water. Cover with plastic wrap (cling film), pierce several times and microwave on High for 2 minutes.

3 Add the couscous to the bowl with the orange juice and 225 ml / 1 cup of boiling water, leave for a few minutes for the liquid to absorb.

4 Add the carrot, bell peppers, cucumber and celery to the couscous and stir to combine.

RATATOUILLE WITH RICE

Ingredients

2 tbsp olive oil

1 onion, chopped

225 g / 8 oz zucchini (courgette, chopped

175 g / 6 oz eggplant (aubergine), chopped

1 clove garlic, crushed

400 g / 14 oz can chopped tomatoes

1 tbsp sun-dried tomato paste

100 g / ½ cup long-grain rice

Method

Prep and cook time: 1 hour

1 Heat the oil in a large skillet. Add the onion and cook gently for 5 minutes to soften (do not brown). Add the zucchini, eggplant and garlic; fry for a few minutes.

2 Stir in the tomatoes and sun-dried tomato paste; cover and simmer for 20 minutes until the vegetables are tender.

3 Meanwhile, put the rice into a pan with 225ml / 1 cup cold salted water. Cover and bring to a boil; reduce the heat and simmer for 15 minutes until the rice is tender and the liquid is absorbed.

4 Serve the ratatouille with the rice.

CHICKEN AND PEPPER FRICASSÉE

Ingredients

2 tbsp olive oil

2 skinless boneless chicken breasts, cut into small pieces

1 onion, chopped

2 carrots, trimmed and chopped

1 red bell pepper, sliced

600 ml / 2½ cups chicken broth (stock)

200 g / 1 cup sweet corn kernels, optional

250 g / 1½ cups couscous

To garnish:

1 scallion (spring onion), chopped

Method

Prep and cook time: 1 hour

1 Heat the oven to 190C (375 F / Gas Mark 5).

2 Heat the oil in a large flameproof casserole, add the chicken and fry for a few minutes to brown. Add the onion and carrots and cook, stirring, for a few minutes to soften. Stir in the red pepper and cook for 2 more minutes.

3 Add the broth (stock) and corn and bring to a boil. Cover and carefully transfer to the oven. Bake for 50 minutes until the chicken and vegetables are tender.

4 Drain off 300 ml / 1¼ cups of the cooking liquid into a bowl and add the couscous. Cover and let stand for a few minutes to allow the couscous to absorb the liquid.

5 Fluff up the couscous with a fork and serve in bowls, topped with the chicken fricassée and garnished with chopped scallion (spring onion).

FISH PIE

Ingredients

800 g / 2 lb starchy potato, peeled and cut into chunks

250 g / 8 oz skinless white fish fillet

250 g / 8 oz skinless smoked haddock fillet

1 small onion, quartered

600 ml / 2½ cups full-fat milk, divided

200 g / 8 oz frozen green peas

100 g / 7 tablespoons butter, divided

50 g / ½ cup all-purpose (plain) flour

Salt and freshly ground pepper, to taste

Pinch freshly grated nutmeg

Method

Prep and cook time: 1 hour

1 Put the potatoes into a large pan of salted water and bring to a boil. Reduce heat and simmer for 20 minutes until tender.

2 Meanwhile, arrange the white fish, smoked haddock and onion in a large skillet; add 475ml / 2 cups of the milk. Bring the milk just to a boil – you will see a few small bubbles. Reduce the heat and simmer for 8 minutes; set aside.

3 Lift the fish into an ovenproof dish. Retain the cooking liquid and discard the onion. Flake the fish into large pieces in the baking dish. Scatter the frozen peas over the fish.

4 To make the sauce, melt 3 tablespoons of the butter in a saucepan; stir in the flour and cook for 1 minute over a moderate heat. Gradually pour in a little of the retained poaching milk, then stir until blended. Continue to add the milk gradually, mixing well until you have a smooth thickened sauce. Remove from the heat, season with salt, pepper and nutmeg, then pour over the fish.

5 Heat the oven to 200C (400F / Gas Mark 8).

6 Drain the potatoes and return to the pan with the remaining butter and milk. Season to taste and mash until smooth and lump free. Spoon the mashed potato all over the fish. Fluff the top with a fork.

7 Bake for 30 minutes until the top is golden.

PASTA SALAD WITH STRAWBERRIES

Ingredients

150 g / 5 oz (2 cups) fusilli

1 tbsp olive oil

2 tsp lemon juice

50 g / 1/3 cup crumbled feta or ricotta cheese

200 g / 1½ cups strawberries, hulled and quartered

Mint leaves, torn

Method

Prep and cook time: 15 min

1 Bring a large pot of salted water to a boil and add the pasta. Cook according to the package instructions, until al dente. Drain in a colander under cold running water. Transfer to a large bowl.

2 Pour over the oil and lemon juice and toss to coat.

3 Divide into 4 serving bowls. Crumble over the cheese, scatter over the strawberries and mint leaves and serve within a couple of hours.

SPINACH AND RICOTTA CANNELLONI

Ingredients

For the sauce:

50 g / 4 tablespoons butter

1 clove garlic, crushed

50 g / ½ cup all-purpose flour

600 ml / 2½ cups milk

1 tbsp grated Parmesan cheese

Salt and freshly ground pepper, to taste

For the cannelloni:

8 cannelloni tubes, ready-made
or dried

250 g / 1 x 10-oz package frozen
spinach, thawed and squeezed dry

150 g / ⅔ cup ricotta

1 egg yolk

1 tbsp grated Parmesan cheese

Method

Prep and cook time: 1 hour

1 Heat the oven to 190C (375F / Gas Mark 5).
Grease a shallow baking dish.

2 If using dried cannelloni, bring a large pot of
salted water to a boil and add the cannelloni. Cook
according to the package instructions, until al dente.
Rinse in a colander under cold running water and
set aside.

3 For the sauce, heat the butter in a saucepan, add
the garlic and stir in the flour. Cook, stirring, for
1 minute, then gradually pour in the milk. Cook,
stirring, until the sauce thickens; set aside.

4 For the filling, in a medium bowl, combine the
spinach and ricotta with the egg yolk and Parmesan
cheese; season with salt and pepper.

5 Spoon the mixture into the cannelloni tubes
and place in the prepared baking dish. Spoon over
the sauce, season with a pinch of salt and sprinkle
with the Parmesan cheese. Bake for 30–40 minutes
until the sauce is bubbling.

Ingredients

For 12 mini pizzas

For the pizza base:

400 g / 4 cups all-purpose (plain) flour

20 g / ¾ oz dried yeast

1 tsp. sugar

1 tsp. salt

240 ml / 1 cup lukewarm water

For the pizza topping:

5 tbsp. olive oil

600 g / 3 cups tomato sauce (passata)

Salt and freshly milled pepper

100 g / 4 oz finely sliced ham or prosciutto

½ a red onion, chopped

200 g / 7 oz mozzarella cheese

2 scallions (spring onion), sliced

Method

Prep and cook time: 45 min plus raising time 1 h 40 min

1 For the pizza base, mix together the flour, yeast, sugar, salt and the lukewarm water. Knead to form a smooth dough, then cover and put in a warm place for about 1 hour to rise. Knead the dough again, cover and leave for 30–40 minutes to rise again.

2 Line a cookie sheet with parchment paper. Divide the pizza dough into 12 balls. Roll out each ball on a floured surface. Place on the cookie sheet and press flat, leaving the edge slightly thicker.

3 Pre-heat the oven to 425°F (220°C / Gas Mark 7). Brush each pizza base with a little of the olive oil, then spread tomato sauce (passata) over the top. Season with salt and pepper.

4 Scatter the ham, onion and scallions (spring onions) over the mini-pizzas and sprinkle the cheese over the top. Bake in the oven for about 8–12 minutes until golden brown.

FISH CRUMBLE

Ingredients

450 g / 1 lb fish fillet, cut into chunks (or tuna chunks if preferred)

100 g / 4 oz medium shrimp (prawns)

250 g / 8 oz mascarpone

1 lemon

For the crumble:

125 g / 1 cup all-purpose (plain) flour

75 g / 5 tbsp butter, cubed

1 tbsp chopped parsley

Method

Prep and cook time: 55 min

1 Heat the oven to 190C (375F / Gas Mark 5). Grease a large baking dish.

2 Arrange the fish and shrimp (prawns) in the dish.

3 Combine the mascarpone with 4 tbsp of cold water and the finely grated zest and juice of the lemon, to taste. Spoon the mascarpone mixture over the fish.

4 Put the flour, butter and parsley together in a food processor, or bowl. Pulse together in the processor, or rub together with your fingertips until the mixture forms crumbs.

5 Sprinkle the crumble mixture evenly over the fish. Bake for 35 minutes, until the crumble is golden.

MEATBALLS
WITH GNOCCHI

Ingredients

225 g / ½ lb minced (ground) pork

225g / ½ lb minced (ground) beef

1 egg, beaten

1 onion, finely chopped

50 g / ¼ cup plain dry breadcrumbs

1 tsp oregano

1 tbsp olive oil

2 cloves garlic, crushed

300 g / 11 oz gnocchi

12 cherry tomatoes

250 g / 8 oz mascarpone

100 ml / ⅓ cup milk

Salt and freshly ground pepper, to taste

25 g / ¼ cup grated cheddar cheese

To garnish:

1 tbsp chopped chives

Method

Prep and cook time: 40 min

1 Heat the oven to 200C (400F / Gas Mark 6). Using your hands, combine pork, beef, egg, onion, breadcrumbs and oregano in a large bowl, then shape into 12 meatballs.

2 Heat the oil in a large skillet and add the meatballs and garlic. Fry for 10 minutes, turning occasionally, until browned all over.

3 Bring a large pan of salted water to a boil. Add the gnocchi, return to the boil and cook for 3 minutes. Drain.

4 Tip the meatballs and garlic into a large shallow baking dish and add the gnocchi and cherry tomatoes.

5 Gently warm the mascarpone in a saucepan with the milk, stirring until smooth. Season to taste with salt and pepper.

6 Pour the mascarpone mixture over the meatballs, gnocchi and tomatoes. Sprinkle evenly with the cheddar cheese. Bake for 20 minutes until thoroughly warmed through. Garnish with chopped chives to serve

FRUITY CHICKEN CURRY

Ingredients

2 tbsp vegetable oil

1 onion, chopped

1 carrot, cut into 8 sticks

1 clove garlic, crushed

2 boneless, skinless chicken breasts, cut into small chunks

1 tbsp korma curry paste

1 tbsp mango chutney

150 ml / $2/3$ cups unsweetened coconut milk

1 eating apple, cored, quartered and roughly chopped

100 g / $2/3$ cup frozen peas

To serve:

8 mini poppadums

Cooked basmati rice

Method

Prep and cook time: 30 min

1 Heat the oil in a skillet and gently fry the onion for a few minutes to soften (do not brown). Add the carrot and garlic and cook 1 minute more.

2 Add the chicken and stir-fry for a few minutes, to brown. Stir in the korma curry paste, mango chutney, coconut milk, apple and 150ml / $2/3$ cup of water. Bring to a boil, reduce heat and simmer for 8 minutes.

3 Add the peas and cook for a further 2 minutes. Serve with mini poppadums and rice.

MACARONI CHEESE WITH HAM

Ingredients

225 g / 8 oz stubby macaroni, such as penne, elbows or fusilli

50 g / 4 tablespoons butter

50 g / ½ cup all-purpose (plain) flour

900 ml / 4 cups milk

225 g / 8 oz Emmental cheese, grated

100 g / 3½ oz wafer-thin ham slices, chopped

½ tsp freshly grated nutmeg

Method

Prep and cook time: 25 min

1 Heat the broiler (grill).

2 Bring a large pot of salted water to a boil and add the pasta. Cook according to the package instructions, until al dente.

3 Meanwhile, melt the butter in a medium nonstick skillet (frying pan). Add the flour and cook, stirring, for 1 minute. Gradually add the milk, whisking all the time to make a smooth sauce. Keep stirring until the sauce is thickened.

4 Drain the macaroni and add to the sauce with the cheese, ham and nutmeg.

5 Pour into an ovenproof dish and broil (grill) for 2–3 minutes, just until top is browned, then serve.

SPAGHETTI BOLOGNESE

Ingredients

250 g / 8 oz lean ground (minced) beef

1 tbsp olive oil

1 onion, chopped

1 carrot, chopped

1 roasted red bell pepper, drained

400 g / 14 oz can plum tomatoes, drained

2 dashes Worcestershire sauce

200 g / 7 oz spaghetti

To garnish:

Basil leaves

Method

Prep and cook time: 40 min

1 Fry the beef in a large nonstick skillet for 15 minutes, until browned.

2 Heat the oil in a large skillet, add the onion and carrot; cook for 5 minutes to soften.

3 Chop the bell pepper and add it to the carrot and onion. Stir in the tomatoes and their juice, and cook for 5 minutes more.

4 Purée the tomato mixture in a blender or food processor until smooth.

5 Add the tomato sauce and Worcestershire sauce to the beef. Add 100 ml / ½ cup of water, stir, cover and simmer for 10 minutes.

6 Meanwhile, bring a large pot of salted water to a boil, add the spaghetti and cook according to package instructions, for about 10 minutes, until al dente.

7 Drain the pasta and divide between 4 plates. Top with the beef mixture and garnish with basil leaves.

BREADED FISH FINGERS

Ingredients

100 g / 1½ cups fresh breadcrumbs

1 tbsp chopped fresh parsley or dill

2 tbsp mayonnaise

3 tbsp all-purpose flour

2 eggs, beaten

450 g / 1 lb skinless cod fillets, cut into finger-size strips

Green peas, to serve

Method

Prep and cook time: 30 min

1 Heat the oven to 220C (400F / Gas Mark 7).

2 Mix the breadcrumbs, parsley or dill and mayonnaise together in a bowl until combined.

3 Place the breadcrumb mixture, flour and beaten egg in 3 separate shallow bowls. Coat each piece of fish first in the flour, shaking off the excess, then dip into the egg and finally, roll in the breadcrumbs.

4 Place the fish fingers on a nonstick baking sheet and bake for 8–10 minutes, until lightly golden and crisp.

5 Meanwhile, cook the peas according to the package directions, and serve with the fish.

PASTA WITH BACON, SHRIMP AND BROCCOLI

Ingredients

200 g / 8 oz penne

100 g / ½ cup broccoli, cut into small florets

2 slices bacon, chopped

8 medium shrimp (prawns)

1 tbsp olive oil spread or olive oil

25 g / ⅓ cup finely grated Parmesan cheese

Method

Prep and cook time: 25 min

1 Bring a large pot of salted water to a boil and add the penne. Cook according to the package instructions, until al dente. Add the broccoli to the pasta water for the last 3 minutes of cooking time.

2 Meanwhile, fry the bacon in a nonstick skillet (frying pan) for about 5 minutes until well cooked. Add the shrimps and cook for 3 more minutes until firm.

3 Drain the pasta and broccoli and put into a large bowl with the bacon and shrimp. Stir in the olive oil spread or drizzle with olive oil; spoon into bowls and sprinkle with Parmesan cheese to serve.

BAKED BROCCOLI RISOTTO

Ingredients

25 g / 2 tbsp butter

1 onion, chopped

300 g / 12 oz risotto rice

150 g / ½ cup broccoli, cut into small florets

700 ml / 3 cups hot vegetable broth (stock)

50 g / ½ cup Cheddar cheese, grated

25 g / 1 oz plain dry breadcrumbs

Method
Prep and cook time: 35 min

1 Heat oven to 200C (400F / Gas Mark 6).

2 Heat the butter in a flameproof casserole. Add the onion and cook, stirring, for 3–4 minutes until softened but not browned.

3 Add the rice and mix well until coated. Add the broccoli and the hot broth (stock), then give the rice a quick stir.

4 Cover with a tightly fitting lid and bake for 15 minutes until just cooked.

5 Stir in the cheese and sprinkle with the breadcrumbs. Return to the oven for a few minutes until crumb topping is golden.

PASTA WITH SPINACH, TOMATOES AND CHICKEN

Ingredients

200 g / 8 oz stubby macaroni, such as penne, ziti or rigatoni

1 tbsp olive oil

1 skinless, boneless chicken breast, cubed

125 ml / ½ cup milk

125 ml / ½ cup light cream

150 g / ½ cup thawed frozen spinach

2 tbsp instant flour (thickening granules)

1 tbsp grated Parmesan cheese

Salt and freshly ground pepper, to taste

8 cherry tomatoes, halved

To garnish:

4 basil leaves

Method

Prep and cook time: 30 min

1 Bring a large pan of salted water to a boil. Add the macaroni and cook according to package instructions, until al dente.

2 Meanwhile, heat the oil in a large skillet. Add the chicken and fry, turning as needed, until cooked through, 10 minutes.

3 Combine the milk, cream and spinach in a medium saucepan; stir in the instant flour (thickening granules), bring to a boil and simmer, stirring, until thickened. Stir in the Parmesan cheese and season with salt and pepper.

4 Drain the macaroni and add to the creamy sauce with the chicken and tomatoes.

6 Serve the pasta in bowls garnished with basil leaves.

QUICK COUSCOUS WITH CHICKEN AND VEGETABLES

Ingredients

1 boneless skinless chicken breast, chopped

300 ml / 1¼ cups water

200 g / 1 cup frozen mixed vegetables, such as peas and carrots, sweetcorn

100 g / ⅔ cup couscous

25 g / 2 tbsp butter

Method

Prep and cook time: 15 min

1 Place the chicken and water in a saucepan; bring to a boil, reduce heat and simmer for 5–8 minutes until the chicken is tender.

2 Add the frozen mixed vegetables and cook for 3 more minutes until the vegetables are tender and the chicken is cooked through.

3 Stir in the couscous, turn off the heat and let stand, covered, for a few minutes, until the liquid is absorbed.

4 Stir in the butter and serve.

POTATO AND CHEESE BAKE

Ingredients

150 ml / ²/₃ cup milk

150 ml / ²/₃ cups heavy (double) cream

450 g / 1 lb even-sized small potatoes, thinly sliced

15 g / 1 tsp butter, chopped

100 g / ½ cup grated Cheddar cheese

½ tsp thyme leaves

Method

Prep and cook time: 1 h 20 min

1 Heat the oven to 200C (400F / Gas Mark 6).

2 Whisk the milk and cream in a medium bowl. Grease a 750 ml / 3-cup baking dish.

3 Arrange a layer of sliced potatoes over the base of the dish, sprinkle with a little butter and cheese. Continue layering, alternating the potatoes with the butter and cheese. Pour over the milk and cream mixture and scatter over the thyme leaves.

4 Cover with foil and bake for 1 hour until the potatoes are tender. Remove the foil and cook for 10 more minutes, until the topping is golden.

GINGERBREAD MEN

Ingredients
For 10 biscuits

3 tbsp firmly packed dark brown sugar

2 tbsp golden syrup or dark corn syrup

1-inch cinnamon stick

½ tsp ground ginger

50 g / 4 tbsp butter, cubed

¼ tsp baking soda (bicarbonate of soda)

125 g / 1 cup + 2 tbsp all-purpose (plain) flour

50 g / 2 oz marzipan

Method
Prep and cook time: 40 min plus 30 min chilling time

1 Heat the oven to 180C (350F / Gas Mark 4). Lightly grease two baking sheets.

2 Put the sugar, syrup, cinnamon, ginger and 1 tsp of water, together in a large saucepan and heat, stirring constantly, until the sugar is dissolved. Remove from the heat, remove the cinnamon stick, and stir in the butter and baking soda (bicarbonate of soda).

3 Gradually stir in the flour to make a smooth, manageable dough. Wrap in plastic wrap (clingfilm) and chill until firm, about 30 minutes.

4 Roll the dough out on a lightly floured surface to 3mm / ⅛ inch thickness and cut out the gingerbread men. Use the end of a small clean paintbrush to press out eyes, a nose, a mouth, buttons and a bow tie.

5 Divide the marzipan into 10 pieces. Roll each into a mini sausage and pinch in the middle, then flatten, to make 'bow ties'.

6 Brush the base of each bow tie with a little water and press into the cookies.

7 Place the cookies 5 cm / 2 inches apart on the baking sheets. Bake for 10–15 minutes or until the biscuits feel firm when lightly pressed with a fingertip.

8 Cool on the baking sheets for a few minutes before transferring them to a wire rack to cool completely.

APPLE MUFFINS

Ingredients
For 12 muffins

225 g / 2 cups all-purpose flour

75 g / ⅓ cup superfine (caster) sugar

2 tsp baking soda (bicarbonate of soda)

1 tsp cinnamon, divided

150 ml / ⅔ cup milk

50 ml / ¼ cup sunflower oil

1 egg

2 apples, peeled, cored and finely chopped

50 g / ¼ cup light brown sugar

Method
Prep and cook time: 35 min

1 Heat the oven to 190C (375F / Gas Mark 5). Line a 12-cup muffin tin with paper liners.

2 Combine the flour, sugar, baking soda (bicarbonate of soda) and ½ tsp of the cinnamon in a large bowl. Add the milk, oil, egg and apples; stir for a few seconds until just combined. Spoon the mixture into the prepared muffin cups.

3 Mix the brown sugar and the remaining ½ tsp cinnamon. Sprinkle over each muffin.

4 Bake for 15–20 minutes until firm and lightly browned.

RICE PUDDING WITH BERRIES

Ingredients

For the baked rice pudding:

75 g / scant ½ cup short-grain rice

600 ml / 2½ cups milk

25 g / 2 tbsp superfine (caster) sugar

For the summer berries:

300 g / 12 oz mixed frozen
summer berries, such as raspberries,
redcurrants and blueberries

50 g / ¼ cup superfine (caster) sugar

Method

Prep and cook time: 1 hour

1 Heat the oven to 170C (325F / Gas Mark 3).
Grease a 900 ml / 1-quart baking dish.

2 Add the rice, milk and sugar. Cover with foil and
bake for 1 hour until the rice is tender.

3 Meanwhile, put the frozen berries into a saucepan
with the sugar and 3 tbsp water. Heat for 5 minutes
until the fruit is tender and the sugar is dissolved.

4 To serve, add the rice pudding to the warm
summer berries.

RASPBERRY AND PLUM CRUMBLE

Ingredients

For the filling:

6 dark red plums, quartered, stones removed and washed

200 g / 1 cup raspberries

75 g / ⅓ cup superfine (caster) sugar

For the crumble:

125 g / heaped 1 cup all-purpose (plain) flour

100 g / 7 tablespoons butter, cut into pieces

100 g / ½ cup firmly packed light brown sugar

To garnish:

1 tbsp sanding (rock) sugar

Method

Prep and cook time: 45 min

1 Heat the oven to 180C (350F / Gas Mark 4).

2 Put the plums, raspberries and caster sugar into a saucepan with 1 tbsp water. Simmer for 5 minutes to soften the fruit.

3 Meanwhile, put the flour and butter into a food processor and whiz until the mixture forms crumbs, or put into a bowl and rub the mixture together with your fingertips. Add the brown sugar and pulse to combine.

4 Spoon the fruit into a shallow medium baking dish. Spoon the crumble mixture on top, sprinkle with sanding (rock) sugar and bake for 20 minutes or until pale golden.

POLENTA WITH CRANBERRIES

Ingredients

125 g / 1 cup fresh or thawed frozen cranberries

50 g / ¼ cup caster (superfine) sugar

450 ml / 2 cups milk

75 g / ⅓ cup polenta (yellow cornmeal)

1 tbsp butter

Method

Prep and cook time: 15 min

1 Put the cranberries in a medium-sized microwave-safe bowl with the sugar and 2 tbsp water. Cover with microwave-safe plastic wrap (clingfilm); pierce a couple of times. Cook on High for 2 minutes or until the cranberries are softened.

2 Put the milk into a saucepan and heat until just below boiling. Gradually add the polenta and cook, stirring constantly, until thickened and smooth.

3 Stir in the butter, remove from the heat and gently stir in the softened cranberries.

BAKED BANANAS
WITH ORANGE
AND COCONUT

Ingredients

4 tsp firmly packed brown sugar

4 tsp butter

2 bananas

1 orange

4 tsp shredded dried coconut

Method

Prep and cook time: 25 min

1 Heat the oven to 350F (180C / Gas Mark 4). Cut 4 x 20-cm / 8-inch squares of foil.

2 Put 1 tsp of sugar in the center of each foil piece, along with 1 tsp butter.

3 Slice the bananas and scatter on top of the butter and sugar mixture.

4 Use a serrated knife to cut away the orange peel and pith. Cut the orange segments away from the orange membrane, catching the juice. Scatter the orange segments over the bananas with the coconut.

5 Gather up the foil edges and pour over any reserved orange juice. Seal each parcel and place on a baking sheet. Bake for 15 minutes to warm through.

FRENCH TOAST WITH BANANA

Ingredients

150 ml / $^2/_3$ cup milk

3 eggs

2 tbsp butter

8 slices whole-wheat bread, shaped into stars with a cutter

3 tbsp caster (superfine) sugar

To garnish:

1 banana

Fresh lemon juice

Method

Prep and cook time: 20 min

1 Put the milk and eggs into a shallow bowl, and beat together with a fork.

2 Heat the butter in a large nonstick skillet (frying pan).

3 Working quickly, dip the bread "stars" into the egg mixture, lift out and place in the skillet. Fry for a couple minutes, then turn them over and cook for another couple of minutes until golden.

4 Sprinkle the French toast with sugar.

5 Arrange 2 stars on each plate. Slice the banana, toss in the lemon juice and garnish the French toast with a few slices of banana.

BIG APPLE PANCAKE

Ingredients

150 g / 1¼ cups all-purpose flour

½ tsp baking soda (baking powder)

3 eggs

150 ml / ⅔ cup buttermilk

2 tbsp sunflower oil

1 apple, peeled and sliced

To garnish:

Fresh mint leaves

Method

Prep and cook time: 20 min

1 Sift the flour and baking soda into a large bowl.

2 In a medium bowl, whisk together the eggs and buttermilk with 3 tbsp cold water.

3 Pour the wet ingredients into the dry and whisk everything together to make a fairly smooth batter (do not overbeat).

4 Heat the oil in a large nonstick skillet and add the apple. Fry gently for several minutes until softened. Turn over the apple pieces.

5 Pour in the pancake batter and cook for about 3 minutes until the underside is firm, then use a large nonstick spatula to flip the pancake. Cook for 3 more minutes, or until the pancake is cooked through.

6 Cut into wedges and serve garnished with mint leaves.

ORANGE AND POMEGRANATE CUPS

Ingredients

1 tbsp powdered unflavored gelatin

100 g / ½ cup superfine (caster) sugar

300 ml / 1⅓ cups orange juice

300 ml / 1⅓ cups pomegranate or apple juice

To garnish:

4 sponge fingers (ladyfingers biscuits)

Method

Prep and cook time: 15 min plus 2 hours chilling

1 Place the gelatin into a heatproof cup and add 2 tbsp boiling water, stirring to dissolve.

2 Combine the sugar and orange juice in a saucepan and heat through, stirring to dissolve the sugar.

3 Add the gelatin mixture; remove from the heat and stir until both the sugar and gelatin is dissolved. Stir in the pomegranate or apple juice. Pour into 4 glasses. Refrigerate for 1 hour to partially set the gelatin.

4 Push a sponge finger into each glass of half-set gelatin and continue to chill until firm.

RHUBARB YOGURT LOLLIES

Ingredients

250 g / 8 oz rhubarb, trimmed and chopped

225 g / 1 heaped cup superfine (caster) sugar

150 ml / ^{2}/3 cup red grape juice

250 g / generous 1 cup full fat natural yogurt

1 lemon, juice squeezed

2 tsp vanilla extract

Method

Prep and cook time: 30 min plus 5 hours freezing time

1 Put the rhubarb, one-third of the sugar and the grape juice into a pan. Simmer gently for 10 minutes. Cool.

2 Mix together the natural yogurt, lemon juice, vanilla extract and the remaining sugar.

3 Spoon the rhubarb mixture into the bases of the 4 popsicle (lolly) molds or espresso cups.

4 Spoon on the yogurt mixture, dividing equally between each.

5 Carefully push a popsicle stick half way down each one. Freeze for 5 hours.

6 Dip the base of each mold in hot water to release the popsicles (lollies) from the molds.

RASPBERRY FROZEN YOGURT

Ingredients

50 g / scant $^1/_3$ cup sifted icing (confectioners') sugar

300 g / 12 oz frozen raspberries

4 tbsp honey

500 g / 1 lb low fat plain yogurt

To garnish:

12 raspberries

Method

Prep and cook time: 20 min plus at least 5 hours freezing time and 20 min defrosting time

1 Put the confectioners' sugar into a food processor with the raspberries and whiz together until smooth, or mash everything together with a potato masher.

2 Add the honey and yogurt and whiz together to combine, or mix with a potato masher. Do not overprocess.

3 Spoon into a freezer-proof container, seal and freeze for several hours.

4 To serve, remove the frozen yogurt from the freezer for 20 minutes to soften slightly. Serve garnished with fresh raspberries.

FRUIT KEBABS WITH CHOCOLATE DRIZZLE

Ingredients

1 kiwi fruit, peeled

2 thick slices fresh pineapple, cored

2 thick slices cantaloupe, seeded

1 thick slice watermelon, seeded

75 g / 2½ oz milk chocolate, (20% cocoa solids) broken into squares

Method
Prep and cook time: 20 min

1 Cut the kiwi fruit into quarters, then halve each piece to make eighths.

2 Cut each pineapple slice into 12 chunks.

3 Cut each cantaloupe melon slice into 6 chunks.

4 Cut the watermelon slice into 12 wedges.

5 Thread alternate pieces of kiwi, pineapple, cantaloupe and watermelon slices onto 8 popsicle (lolly) sticks.

6 In a small microwave-safe bowl, microwave the chocolate on Medium power, stirring every 30 seconds, until just melted. Drizzle the chocolate over the fruit kebabs.

STAR COOKIES

Ingredients

For 12 cookies

250 g / 2 cups all-purpose (plain) flour

90 g / scant ½ cup superfine (caster) sugar

175 g / 12 tablespoons (1½ sticks) butter, cubed

12 candy-coated chocolate pieces

Method

Prep and cook time: 30 min

1 Heat the oven to 180C (350F /Gas Mark 4).

2 Put the flour, sugar and butter together in a processor and blend together to make crumbs, or put into a bowl and rub everything together with your fingertips. Pulse a little more to form into a ball, or squeeze the mixture together with your hands.

3 Turn the dough onto a sheet of parchment paper. Use a lightly floured rolling pin to roll out the dough to 0.5 cm / ¼-inch thickness.

4 Dip a 10 cm / 4-inch star cutter in flour and stamp out 10 star shapes, carefully removing the trimmings from around the sides, but leaving the cookies on the paper. Reroll the trimmings to make 2 additional cookies.

5 Place the dough, still on the parchment, onto 2 baking sheets. Press a candy into the center of each. Bake for 10 minutes until pale golden. Cool and store in an airtight tin.

PANCAKES WITH RASPBERRIES AND MAPLE SYRUP

Ingredients

125 g / 1 cup + 2 tbsp all-purpose flour

2 eggs

200 ml / ¾ cup + 2 tbsp milk

2 tbsp vegetable oil

200 g / 1 cup raspberries

4 tbsp maple syrup

Method

Prep and cook time: 20 min

1 Put the flour in a bowl, then gradually whisk in the eggs and milk until smooth. (This can also be done in a food processor.)

2 Heat a thin layer of oil in a nonstick skillet or griddle until a drop of water skitters when dripped on the surface. Add 3 tbsp of the batter to the pan, swirling to coat the base of the pan.

3 Cook the pancake for 2 minutes until firm and golden brown underneath, then use a nonstick spatula to flip the pancake over. Cook for 1 minute more.

4 Slide the pancake onto a warm plate. Continue with the rest of the batter, stacking the finished pancakes between sheets of wax paper, so they don't stick together.

5 Use a flower or star-shaped cutter to stamp out shaped pancakes, if desired. Serve with raspberries, drizzled with maple syrup.

Published by Transatlantic Press

First published in 2011

Transatlantic Press
38 Copthorne Road, Croxley Green, Hertfordshire WD3 4AQ

© Transatlantic Press

Images and Recipes by StockFood © The Food Image Agency

Recipes selected by Jonnie Léger, StockFood

A catalogue record for this book is available from the British Library.

ISBN 978-1-907176-40-1

Printed in China